italian breads

italian breads
from focaccia to grissini

with recipes by
Maxine Clark

RYLAND
PETERS
& SMALL

LONDON NEW YORK

Designer Iona Hoyle
Commissioning Editor Julia Charles
Production Controller Toby Marshall
Art Director Leslie Harrington
Publishing Director Alison Starling

Indexer Hilary Bird

First published in the
United States in 2009
by Ryland Peters & Small, Inc.
519 Broadway, 5th Floor
New York, NY 10012
www.rylandpeters.com

10 9 8 7 6 5 4 3 2 1

Text © Maxine Clark,
Linda Collister, Liz Franklin 2009
Design and photographs
© Ryland Peters & Small 2009

Library of Congress Cataloging-in-Publication Data
Clark, Maxine, 1955-
    Italian breads : from focaccia to grissini :
      with recipes / by Maxine Clark.
        p. cm.
    Includes index.
    ISBN 978-1-84597-900-3
    1. Bread–Italy. 2. Cookery, Italian. I. Title.
    TX769.C52 2009
    641.5945–dc22

                                        2009008744

Printed in China

Notes
• All spoon measurements given are level
unless otherwise specified.
• Eggs used in the recipes are large
unless otherwise specified.
• All dough rising times given are
approximate as they will depend on the
consistency of the dough and the ambient
temperature. There may also be slight
variants in water quantities depending on
the humidity and the absorption qualities
of the flour being used.
• Ovens should be preheated to the
specified temperatures. All ovens work
slightly differently. We recommend using
an oven thermometer and suggest you
consult the maker's handbook for any
special instructions, particularly if you are
cooking in a fan-assisted oven, as you will
need to adjust temperatures according to
manufacturer's instructions.

contents

introduction

Nothing smells as good as freshly-baked bread still warm from the oven. Baking your own at home is a hugely enjoyable and satisfying process—with basic ingredients, simple equipment, and the recipes given in this book, you will be able to make a variety of delicious Italian-style loaves and rolls to enjoy every day.

The main ingredients necessary to make Mediterranean-style breads are flour, salt, yeast, and water, though they are often enriched with flavorsome ingredients such as olives, nuts, or dried fruits. Choosing the right flour is important for a good result. Throughout Italy, *Farina de Grano Tenero* is used for breadmaking—this is the finest, whitest grade of soft wheat flour. "0" indicates the grade of the flour, "00" being the finest. Do shop around to find it.

Yeast is available fresh or dried and it's really up to you which you prefer to buy. Whatever yeast you use, it needs moisture and warmth to develop. Make sure the liquid is at the correct temperature—too cold and the dough will rise slowly; too hot and you risk killing the yeast. When a recipe states "hand-hot water" it should be between 105°F and 115°F. Also, the softer the water, the better the dough, so I like to use filtered or bottled water. Breads, such as focaccia, rely heavily on olive oil for their flavor, so do use extra virgin olive oil. It need not be an expensive one—most supermarket blends are fine.

As far as equipment goes, you should have a good selection of mixing bowls, measuring spoons, measuring cups, weighing scales, and a sharp knife or pastry wheel for cutting dough. My favorite gadget is a pastry scraper which can be used as a knife, scoop, and board scraper. A steady work surface at the right height is essential for energetic kneading. This surface should be able to cope with sticky dough, flour, and olive oil and be easy to clean. A flour shaker is also useful; an olive oil pourer will let you drizzle small amounts of oil; and a water spray mists dough with just enough water to keep it moist and is essential kit.

For baking, you will need deep, heavy metal pans for deep-pan focaccias, heavy rectangular pans for larger loaves, and good, heavy rimless baking sheets for pizzas and flatbreads. Pans with a non-stick surface tend to "stew" doughs so I prefer to use metal, iron, or heavy aluminium. Some recipes suggest using a testo—this is a type of bakestone that is heated in the oven for at least 30 minutes before starting to bake and mimics the base of a real pizza oven. When the dough comes into contact with the stone, the moisture is absorbed and the heat evenly distributed. It's a good investment if you intend to make a lot of pizzas and flatbreads but a sturdy baking sheet will also do the job. So roll up your sleeves and start bread-making today—once you've tasted your own loaves I guarantee you'll never want to buy lack-lustre supermarket bread again!

loaves and rolls

This is almost an Italian equivalent of garlic bread, but much better. You can use ordinary pizza dough, or enrich it with egg. The thin dough base is smothered in pesto and green olives, rolled up to look like a long jelly roll and left to rise again. Drenched in garlic oil and smothered in pecorino cheese, the smell alone wafting from the oven is to die for!

rolled pesto, olive, and garlic bread

4¼ cups Italian "00" flour or unbleached all-purpose flour

1 teaspoon sugar

½ teaspoon fine sea salt

1 cake compressed yeast, 1 package active dry yeast, or 2 teaspoons quick-rising dry yeast

1 egg, beaten

3 tablespoons extra virgin olive oil

1⅔ cups hand-hot water

1 cup fresh pesto

7 oz. large green olives, pitted and roughly chopped

3 cups freshly grated pecorino or Parmesan cheese

2–3 tablespoons garlic-infused olive oil

sea salt and freshly ground black pepper

a rimless baking sheet

a terra cotta bakestone or a large, heavy baking sheet

makes 1 medium loaf

Sift the flour, sugar, and salt into a large bowl and make a well in the center. Crumble in the compressed yeast or sprinkle in the active dry yeast, if using. If you are using quick-rising dry yeast, follow the manufacturer's instructions. Rub in the yeast until the mixture resembles fine bread crumbs. Pour in the beaten egg, olive oil, and hand-hot water and mix until the dough comes together. Knead the dough energetically on a floured work surface for 5 minutes until soft, smooth, and elastic. Put it in a lightly-oiled bowl, cover with plastic wrap or a damp kitchen towel and let rise in a warm place until doubled in size—about 1½ hours.

Preheat the oven to 400°F. Put the bakestone or heavy baking sheet in the oven to heat up.

When risen, knock back the dough, then roll or pull into a large rectangle as thinly as you can, directly onto a sheet of baking parchment. Spread the dough liberally with the pesto, leaving a ½-inch rim all around the dough, then scatter over the olives and 1¾ cups of the pecorino. Season. Using the baking parchment, roll the dough up like a jelly roll, starting from the long side. Slide the dough onto another sheet of baking parchment making sure the seam is underneath. Brush with the garlic oil and sprinkle with the remaining pecorino.

Slide the rolled bread onto the rimless baking sheet. Working quickly, open the oven door and slide both paper and bread onto the hot bakestone or baking sheet.

Bake in the preheated oven for 20 minutes, then carefully slide out the baking parchment. Bake for a further 5 minutes until the crust is golden. Remove from the oven and serve warm (not hot) or cold in slices.

This is an unyeasted bread from Umbria, and very quick to rustle up. When making this type of bread, work quickly, because as soon as the liquid comes into contact with the baking powder, a chemical reaction starts to aerate the bread. Use a light hand and get the dough into the oven as soon as possible.

Parmesan soda bread

2⅔ cups Italian "00" flour or cake flour

1 teaspoon baking powder

1 teaspoon fine sea salt

½ cup freshly grated Parmesan cheese, plus extra to dust

3 tablespoons butter, melted and cooled

½–⅔ cup milk

2 eggs

a testo, terra cotta bakestone, or a large, heavy baking sheet

a rimless baking sheet, lined with baking parchment

makes 1 medium loaf

Put the testo, terra cotta bakestone, or a large, heavy baking sheet on the lower shelf of the oven. Preheat the oven to 375°F for at least 30 minutes.

Sift the flour, baking powder, and salt into a medium mixing bowl. Stir in the Parmesan and make a well in the center.

Whisk the cooled, melted butter with ½ cup of the milk and the eggs, and pour into the well. Mix until just combined—overmixing will make the bread tough. The dough should be quite soft; if it isn't, add a little more milk. Turn out onto a floured work surface and knead briefly. Put the ball of dough directly onto a rimless baking sheet lined with baking parchment. Pat into a disk about 1¼ inches thick. Brush with a little milk, then mark into wedges with the back of a knife and dust with Parmesan.

Working quickly, open the oven door and slide both baking parchment and bread onto the hot testo, bakestone, or baking sheet. If you are brave, try to shoot the bread into the oven leaving the baking parchment behind—this takes practice!

Bake for 15 minutes, then very carefully slide out and remove the baking parchment. Bake for a further 5 minutes or until the crust is really golden. Remove from the oven and wrap in a clean kitchen towel. Serve warm, broken into wedges, ready to split and fill.

This is a simple yet delicious rustic loaf flavored with fresh sage. It is particularly good served warm from the oven and is the perfect accompaniment to hearty winter soups and stews. It works particularly well with pumpkin or butternut squash dishes as the musky sage complements their sweetness perfectly.

Tuscan fresh sage and olive oil bread

3 cups unbleached all-purpose flour

1 cup whole-wheat flour

2 teaspoons freshly chopped sage leaves

1 tablespoon baking powder

½ teaspoon fine sea salt

2 large eggs

3 tablespoons olive oil

about ¾ cup milk

a baking sheet, lightly greased

makes 1 medium loaf

Preheat the oven to 350°F.

Mix the flours with the chopped sage leaves, baking powder, and salt in a large bowl.

In a separate bowl, lightly beat the eggs with the olive oil and milk, then stir into the dry ingredients to make a soft and slightly sticky dough. If there are dry crumbs or the dough feels stiff, work in a little more milk.

Turn out the dough onto a lightly-floured work surface and shape into a ball about 7 inches across. Put it on the prepared baking sheet and score the top with a sharp knife.

Put in the oven immediately and bake for about 45 minutes or until golden brown and the loaf sounds hollow when tapped underneath with your knuckles. Transfer to a wire rack and leave until cool enough to break into quarters or cut into thick slices. This loaf is best eaten the same day but can be frozen for up to 1 month.

variation:
To make an Olive and Rosemary Bread, follow the same method as above, replacing the sage with 1 teaspoon freshly chopped rosemary needles and adding ½ cup roughly chopped pitted black and green olives.

Ciabatta comes from Northern Italy and has become almost as popular and ubiquitous as the baguette. It has a floury crust, a moist open texture, and a good flavor of fruity olive oil. For the best results, use an Italian ciabatta flour, which is granular and quite coarse in texture. This helps create a lively dough producing the large air bubbles needed for the characteristic texture.

ciabatta rolls

1⅓ cups hand-hot water

1 cake compressed yeast*

3¼ cups Italian ciabatta flour or unbleached all-purpose flour

2 teaspoons fine sea salt

¼ cup extra virgin olive oil

For the biga (aged-dough starter):

1¾ cups all-purpose flour

⅓ cake compressed yeast*

⅔ cup hand-hot water

2 baking sheets, heavily floured

makes 12 rolls

* If using active dry yeast, mix one-third of a ¼-oz. package with the flour to make the biga, then work in the water. Finish the biga as in the main recipe. To make the ciabatta dough, add the water to the biga and work in to make a batter. Then mix half the flour with one ¼-oz. package of active dry yeast, add to the batter, and finish as in the main recipe.

To make the biga, put the flour in a large bowl and make a well in the center. Crumble the yeast into the well, then pour in the hand-hot water. Mix the yeast with the water, then gradually work in the flour to make a firm dough. Turn out onto a lightly-floured work surface and knead for 2 minutes, then return the dough to the bowl and cover. Leave at room temperature for 8–12 hours—it will rise enormously, then fall back.

The next day, to make the ciabatta dough, put the hand-hot water in a bowl and crumble the yeast over the top. Stir well until dispersed. Add to the biga and work into the dough by stirring and squeezing with your fingers to make a thick, smooth batter. Work in half the flour to make a very sticky, batter-like dough, then beat with your hand for 5 minutes until the dough has been thoroughly stretched and become very elastic. Cover the bowl and let rise in a warm place until about 2½ times its original size, about 2 hours.

Add the salt and olive oil to the dough, then gradually work in the rest of the flour to make a rather soft, sticky dough. When the dough feels smooth and very elastic, cover the bowl and let rise in a warm place as before, this time until doubled in size, about 1 hour.

Preheat the oven to 450°F. Put the baking sheets in the oven to heat up.

Gently tip the dough onto a well-floured work surface. Using a floured bread scraper, divide the dough into 12 pieces and transfer to the sheets, spacing well apart. Shape into rough-looking rolls with well-floured fingers. Dust heavily with flour, then slip the sheets into large plastic bags, slightly inflated. Let rise in a warm place for about 30 minutes until almost doubled in size—don't worry if the dough also spreads out. Uncover the rolls, then bake in the preheated oven for 15–20 minutes, until golden brown. Cool on a wire rack. Eat warm from the oven or within 1 day.

These are delicious little savory rolls made just like British Chelsea buns and baked together in a pan. Take the whole lot to the dinner table and break off your own little roll. Perfect with drinks on a warm summer's night, or instead of bread—they will disappear very fast!

walnut and parsley rolls

1 recipe Basic Pizza Dough
(page 18)

1½ cups walnut pieces

a large handful of fresh flatleaf
parsley leaves

2 garlic cloves

⅓ cup extra virgin olive oil

sea salt and freshly ground
black pepper

*a deep pizza pan
or springform cake pan, 9 inches
diameter, lightly oiled*

makes about 20 small rolls

Preheat the oven to 400°F.

Put the walnuts, parsley, and garlic in a food processor and process until evenly chopped. While the machine is running, pour in the olive oil. Season to taste.

Uncover the dough, punch out the air and roll or pull it into a rectangle, 24 x 10 inches, directly onto a large sheet of baking parchment.

Spread the walnut mixture evenly over the dough. Season with salt and pepper. Using the baking parchment, roll the dough up like a jelly roll, starting from the long side. Slide the dough onto another sheet of baking parchment making sure the seam is underneath. Using a large and very sharp knife, cut the roll into 20 even pieces. Cut the dough quickly and smoothly each time—don't saw it or it will stick! Arrange the rolls cut-side up in the prepared pizza pan, spacing them close together but not quite touching. Cover with plastic wrap or a damp kitchen towel and let rise in a warm place for 30 minutes, until the dough has risen to the top of the pan.

Remove the plastic wrap and bake the rolls for 35–45 minutes or until golden. Let cool in the pan if you want them very soft, or turn them out onto a wire rack to cool if you'd like them drier. Serve warm.

Having a recipe for a good basic pizza dough is essential. This will make the typical Neapolitan pizza base—soft and chewy with a crisp crust or cornicione, or it can be used as the basis of a number other recipes throughout the book. I find 1 cup water usually works for me, but if your flour has been kept in dry conditions, it may need a drop more to make a soft dough.

basic pizza dough

1 cake compressed yeast,
1 package active dry yeast, or
2 teaspoons quick-rising dry yeast

½ teaspoon sugar

1 cup hand-hot water

4 cups Italian "0" flour or
unbleached all-purpose flour

1 teaspoon fine sea salt

1 tablespoon olive oil

makes 2 medium-crust
pizza bases, each
10-12 inches diameter

In a medium bowl, cream the compressed yeast with the sugar and beat in the hand-hot water. Leave for 10 minutes until frothy. For other yeasts, follow the manufacturer's instructions.

Sift the flour and salt into a large bowl and make a well in the center. Pour in the yeast mixture, then the olive oil. Mix together with a round-bladed knife, then use your hands until the dough comes together. Tip out onto a lightly-floured work surface, wash and dry your hands, then knead the dough briskly for 5–10 minutes until smooth, shiny, and elastic—5 minutes for warm hands, 10 minutes for cold hands! Don't add extra flour at this stage—a wetter dough is better. If you feel the dough is sticky, lightly flour your hands, not the dough. The dough should be quite soft. If it is really too soft, knead in a little more flour.

To test if the dough is ready, roll it into a fat sausage, take each end in either hand, lift the dough up and stretch the dough outwards, gently wiggling it up and down—it should stretch out quite easily. If it doesn't, it needs more kneading. Shape the dough into a neat ball. Put it in an oiled bowl, cover with plastic wrap or a damp kitchen towel and let rise in a warm place until doubled in size—about 1½ hours.

Uncover the dough, punch out the air, then tip out onto a lightly-floured work surface. Divide into 2 and shape into smooth balls. Place the balls well apart on baking parchment, cover loosely with plastic wrap and let rise in a warm place for 60–90 minutes. Use as required.

focaccia and flatbreads

The word focaccia means a bread baked directly on the hearth, and derives from the Latin word for "hearth" (focus). Although a rustic focaccia can be made with any basic pizza dough, the secret of a truly light, thick focaccia lies in giving the dough three risings, and dimpling the dough so that it traps olive oil while it bakes.

deep-pan focaccia

6⅓ cups Italian "00" flour or cake flour

½ teaspoon fine sea salt

1 cake compressed yeast, 1 package active dry yeast, or 2 teaspoons quick-rising dry yeast

⅔ cup extra virgin olive oil

1¾–2 cups hand-hot water

coarse sea salt or rock salt, to sprinkle

fresh rosemary sprigs (optional)

2 cake, pie, or pizza pans, 10 x 1½ inches diameter, lightly oiled

makes 2 deep focaccias

Sift the flour and fine sea salt into a large bowl and make a well in the center. Crumble in the compressed yeast, or add active dry yeast, if using. If you are using quick-rising dry yeast, follow the manufacturer's instructions. Pour in 6 tablespoons of the olive oil, then rub in the yeast until the mixture resembles fine bread crumbs. Pour in the hand-hot water and mix together with your hands until the dough comes together.

Tip the dough out onto a floured work surface. Wash and dry your hands and knead the dough energetically for 10 minutes until smooth and elastic. The dough should be very soft. Put the dough in a lightly-oiled bowl, cover with plastic wrap or a damp kitchen towel and let rise in a warm place until doubled in size—about 1½ hours.

Uncover the dough, punch out the air and divide into 2. Shape each piece into a round ball on a lightly-floured work surface and roll out into two 10-inch circles and place in the pans. Cover with plastic wrap or a damp kitchen towel and let rise in a warm place for 30 minutes.

Preheat the oven to 400°F.

Uncover the dough. Push your fingertips into the dough right down to the base of the pan to make deep dimples all over the surface. The dough will deflate slightly. Drizzle very generously with olive oil (about ⅓ cup). Sprinkle with coarse sea salt and top with sprigs of rosemary (if using). Re-cover with plastic wrap or a damp kitchen towel, put in a warm place and leave the dough to rise to the top of the pans—about 30 minutes.

Spray the focaccias with water and bake in the preheated oven for about 20–25 minutes, until risen and golden. Drizzle with the remaining olive oil, then transfer to a wire rack to cool.

Eat on the same day or let cool, then wrap up and freeze. When you remove the focaccia from the freezer, thaw and wrap in foil, then reheat for 5 minutes in a hot oven.

This is a wonderful example of the traditional focaccia, as it is baked directly on the bakestone or on a hot baking sheet. If the base is floured very well the focaccia can be slipped directly onto the stone or baking sheet, leaving the baking parchment behind. This is the kind of focaccia that you tear and dip into yet more fruity olive oil.

thin focaccia

1 recipe Deep-Pan Focaccia (page 21), risen twice but uncooked

⅓ cup extra virgin olive oil

coarse sea salt or rock salt, to sprinkle

2 testi, terra cotta bakestones, or large, heavy baking sheets

2 rimless baking sheets, lined with baking parchment

makes 2 large, thin focaccias

Put the 2 testi, terra cotta bakestones, or large, heavy baking sheets on the lower shelf of the oven. Preheat the oven to 425°F for at least 30 minutes.

Uncover the dough, punch out the air, and divide into 2. Shape each piece into a rough ball, then pull and stretch each ball of dough to a large oval shape—as large as will fit in your oven. Put each one on a rimless baking sheet. Cover with lightly-oiled plastic wrap or a damp kitchen towel and leave to rise for 30 minutes.

Remove the plastic wrap and, using your fingertips, make deep dimples all over the surface of the dough right down to the baking sheet. Drizzle over all but 2 tablespoons of the remaining oil. Spray the focaccias with water and sprinkle generously with coarse sea salt. Working quickly, open the oven door and slide the baking parchment and focaccia onto the hot bakestones or baking sheets.

Bake for 15 minutes, then very carefully slide out and remove the baking parchment. Bake the focaccia for a further 15 minutes or until the crust is golden. Brush or drizzle with the remaining olive oil, then transfer to a wire rack to cool.

Eat on the same day or let cool, then wrap up and freeze. When you remove it from the freezer, thaw and wrap in foil, then reheat for 5 minutes in a hot oven.

Use this spicy focaccia to make delicious sandwiches or serve it in thick slices spread with cool, fresh ricotta. Replacing some of the liquid in the dough with tomato paste (or even all the water with tomato juice) gives it a beautiful, rusty red color, studded with bright red cherry peppers and dark chunks of salami or chorizo.

fiery focaccia

½ recipe Deep-Pan Focaccia (page 21), making the changes stated in this recipe

4 tablespoons tomato paste

4–6 red cherry peppers or Peppadews, diced

2 red bell peppers, roasted, seeded, and diced

4 oz. salami or chorizo, cubed

2½ oz. provolone, Emmental, or Gruyère cheese, cubed

⅓ cup extra virgin olive oil, plus extra to brush

coarse sea salt or rock salt, to sprinkle

freshly ground black pepper

a cake or pizza pan, 10 x 1½ inches diameter, lightly oiled

makes 1 focaccia

Make the focaccia dough following the recipe on page 21, but using 4 tablespoons tomato paste dissolved in the water. Knead the dough and give it the first rising.

Uncover the dough, punch out the air, and pull or roll it out into a rough circle. Dot with the cherry peppers, red bell peppers, salami, provolone, and lots of freshly ground black pepper. Flip one half of the dough over and lightly knead to incorporate the ingredients. Shape into a rough ball on a lightly-floured surface and pat into the prepared pan. Cover lightly with plastic wrap or a damp kitchen towel and let rise in a warm place for 30 minutes.

Remove the plastic wrap and, using your fingertips, make deep dimples all over the surface of the dough. Drizzle over the olive oil, re-cover very lightly with plastic wrap and let rise for a final 30 minutes until very puffy.

Preheat the oven to 400°F.

Uncover the focaccia, spray with water, and sprinkle generously with coarse sea salt. Bake for 20–25 minutes, until risen and golden. Transfer to a wire rack, brush with olive oil, and let cool.

Eat on the same day or let cool, then wrap up and freeze. When you remove it from the freezer, thaw and wrap in foil, then reheat for 5 minutes in a hot oven.

This is an unusual bread from the coastal areas of Lunigiana, made from a mixture of cornmeal and wheat flour. It is traditionally made between November and the end of January to coincide with the olive harvest and cooked in a wood-fired oven on a bed of chestnut leaves. I had some on a recent visit there—my friend's boyfriend made it in a bread oven outside on the terrace.

cornmeal and olive focaccia with rosemary and sage

4¼ cups Italian "00" flour or cake flour

2¼ cups fine polenta flour (*farina gialla* or *granoturco*)

2 packages quick-rising dry yeast

7 oz. black olives, pitted and halved

3 tablespoons pine nuts

2 tablespoons freshly chopped sage

2 tablespoons freshly chopped rosemary needles

2–3 garlic cloves, finely chopped

3 tablespoons extra virgin olive oil, plus extra to drizzle

2 cups hand-hot water

coarse sea salt or rock salt, to sprinkle

freshly ground black pepper

a jelly roll pan, 13 x 9 inches, oiled

makes 1 large focaccia

Mix the flours and yeast in a large bowl. Add the olives, pine nuts, sage, rosemary, and garlic, then mix. Make a well in the center and add the olive oil mixed with the hand-hot water. Mix to a very soft dough, turn out onto a lightly-floured work surface and knead very vigorously for 10 minutes.

Roll or pull the dough into a rectangle to fit the jelly roll pan, pushing the dough into the corners. Cover with plastic wrap or a damp kitchen towel and let rise in a warm place for about 20–30 minutes until quite puffy.

Preheat the oven to 400°F.

Using your fingertips, make deep dimples all over the dough and drizzle with olive oil. Sprinkle with coarse sea salt and grind over some black pepper. Bake for about 35 minutes, until risen, firm, and dark golden.

Eat on the same day or let cool, then wrap up and freeze. When you remove it from the freezer, thaw and wrap in foil, then reheat for 5 minutes in a hot oven.

Making a bread by mixing mashed potatoes with flour and anointing it lavishly with good olive oil is common all over Italy, especially in Liguria and Puglia, where some of the best olive oil comes from. It is delicious, but quite dense. I tend not to pit the olives for this as they can dry out too much in the oven but don't forget to warn whoever is eating it before serving.

potato and olive focaccia

1 lb. floury baking potatoes, unpeeled

5¼ cups Italian "00" flour or cake flour

½ teaspoon fine sea salt

1 cake compressed yeast, 1 package active dry yeast, or 2 teaspoons quick-rising dry yeast

7 oz. large, juicy green olives, with pits in

⅔ cup extra virgin olive oil

coarse sea salt or rock salt, to sprinkle

2 cake pans, 10 x 1½ inches, or a large rectangular roasting pan, lightly oiled

makes 2 medium focaccias

Boil or bake the potatoes in their skins and peel them whilst still warm. Mash them or pass them through a potato ricer.

Sift the flour with the fine sea salt into a large bowl and make a well in the center. Crumble in the compressed yeast, or add the active dry yeast, if using. If you are using quick-rising dry yeast, follow the manufacturer's instructions. Add the potatoes and mix together with your hands until the dough comes together. Tip the dough out onto a floured work surface, wash and dry your hands. Knead the dough energetically for 10 minutes until smooth and elastic. The dough should be soft; if it isn't, add a couple of tablespoons of warm water.

Divide the dough into 2, shape each piece into a round ball on a lightly-floured surface and roll out into two 10-inch circles or a large rectangle to fit whichever pans you are using. Put the dough in the pans, cover with plastic wrap or a damp kitchen towel and let rise in a warm place for 2 hours.

Preheat the oven to 400°F.

Uncover the dough, scatter over the olives, and, using your fingertips, make deep dimples all over the surface of the dough, pushing in some of the olives here and there. Drizzle with ⅓ cup of the olive oil, re-cover, and let rise for another 30 minutes.

Uncover the dough, spray with water, and sprinkle generously with coarse sea salt. Bake for 20–25 minutes until risen and golden brown. Brush or drizzle with the remaining olive oil, then transfer to a wire rack to cool.

Eat on the same day, or let cool, then wrap up and freeze. When you remove the focaccia from the freezer, thaw and wrap in foil, then reheat for 5 minutes in a hot oven.

When I was teaching in Italy, I made focaccia in all shapes and sizes, and with many different flours. I wondered how it would taste if I incorporated my native oat flour. I decided to use fine oat flour and "00" flour and to scatter rolled oats and salt on top. The result was a thin, crisp, but still moist focaccia, with a golden, crunchy topping.

oatmeal focaccia

1 package active dry yeast

1 teaspoon sugar

1⅔–2 cups hand-hot water

1 cup oat flour, warmed

4¼ cups Italian "00" flour or cake flour, warmed

2 teaspoons English mustard powder

1 teaspoon freshly ground black pepper

2 teaspoons fine sea salt

2 tablespoons extra virgin olive oil, plus extra to drizzle

3–4 tablespoons old-fashioned rolled oats

coarse sea salt or rock salt, to sprinkle

2 jelly roll pans, 9 x 13 inches, oiled

makes 2 thin focaccias

Whisk the yeast and sugar into the hand-hot water and stir in the oat flour. Cover and let stand in a warm place for 10–15 minutes until frothy.

Sift the flour, mustard powder, pepper, and fine sea salt into a warm bowl, pour in the oat flour mixture and add the olive oil. Mix to a soft dough. Add a little extra warm water if the dough looks too dry. Turn out and knead for at least 10 minutes or until elastic.

Place in a lightly-oiled bowl, cover with plastic wrap or a damp kitchen towel and let rise in a warm place for about 1 hour or until doubled in size.

Uncover the dough, punch out the air and divide into 2 pieces. Pull and roll each piece to fit the jelly roll pans. Put in the pans and press into the corners. Prick the dough all over with a fork and scatter the rolled oats and coarse sea salt over the top. Cover with oiled plastic wrap or a damp kitchen towel and let rise in a warm place until puffy—about 30–60 minutes.

Preheat the oven to 400°F.

Drizzle the focaccia with olive oil and bake for 25 minutes, until golden. Remove from the oven and drizzle with a little more olive oil. Cool on a wire rack and serve cut into thin fingers. Best eaten the same day.

In Italy these flatbreads are known as piadine (a piadina is a "little plate") and are traditionally cooked on a testo (a thick, flat piece of terra cotta). As these are difficult to buy outside Italy, I use unglazed terra cotta plant-pot saucers with great success. Never oil a testo—it must be clean and dry. Keep the piadine warm and soft inside a folded napkin in a basket until they are ready to serve. Serve them warm, folded over, with thinly sliced prosciutto or salami piled inside.

flatbreads from Emilia Romagna

4¼ cups Italian "00" flour or unbleached all-purpose flour

1 teaspoon baking powder

a pinch of fine sea salt

¼ cup good olive oil, melted unsalted butter, or pure lard

¾ cup hand-hot water

a testo, iron girdle, or heavy-based skillet

makes about 8 flatbreads

Sift the flour, baking powder, and salt into a large bowl. Make a well in the center, pour in the olive oil and the hand-hot water and mix to make a soft dough. Add more water if the dough looks a little dry. Knead for a couple of minutes or until smooth, wrap in plastic wrap and let rest at room temperature for 30 minutes.

Divide the dough into 8, keeping the pieces covered under a large upturned bowl. Roll each into a thin 8-inch disk. Stack these up with baking parchment or plastic wrap between each, and cover with plastic wrap or a damp kitchen towel.

Heat the testo on the stovetop until medium hot. Slide a disk of dough onto the hot testo and cook for about 30–40 seconds until brown spots appear on the underside. Flip it over and cook for a further 30 seconds or until both sides are dry-looking and covered with brown spots or blisters (like a Mexican tortilla or Indian chappati). Avoid cooking them for too long as they will end up being dry and tough.

Keep the cooked piadine warm and soft inside a folded napkin or loosely wrapped in foil in a warm oven, while you are cooking the remainder. They are best served warm and eaten on the same day.

This Ligurian speciality should be made with very good olive oil. It is traditionally baked in a large, shallow copper pan, but a wide metal pizza pan will do. The batter itself can be flavored with chopped rosemary needles, dried chile, or black pepper. If you can't find Italian chickpea flour, use Indian gram flour (available in Asian markets) although the color will be paler.

chickpea and rosemary flatbread

¼ cup extra virgin olive oil

1⅔ cups Italian chickpea flour (*farina di ceci*) or Indian gram flour

1 teaspoon fine sea salt

needles from 4 fresh rosemary sprigs

sea salt flakes and cracked black pepper, to sprinkle

a pizza pan or shallow cake pan, 11 inches diameter

makes 1 large flatbread

Put 2 cups cold water in a bowl with 1 tablespoon of the olive oil. Gradually whisk in the chickpea flour and fine sea salt until smooth and creamy. Cover and let stand for at least 30 minutes, or overnight in the refrigerator if possible.

Preheat the oven to 450°F.

Grease the pizza pan with the remaining olive oil. It must be well oiled to give the right flavor and ensure a crisp edge.

Stir the batter and pour it into the prepared pizza pan. Sprinkle the rosemary on top and bake for about 20 minutes or until set and golden.

Serve warm, cut into slices or lozenge shapes, and sprinkled with salt flakes and cracked black pepper. Best eaten on the same day.

savory bites

These little flatbreads are made with cornmeal and wheat flour. They are similar to English muffins and are served at local festivals in the Lunigiana, Tuscany. Cooked on a girdle and ready in minutes, they are golden and puffy, and smell delicious. Serve split and filled with cheese, alongside a selection of cold meats and salami.

cornmeal muffins

1 cake compressed yeast,
1 package active dry yeast, or
2 teaspoons quick-rising dry yeast

1 teaspoon sugar

1¾ cups hand-hot water

4¼ Italian "00" flour or
cake flour

1⅔ cups fine cornmeal or polenta

1½ teaspoons fine sea salt

6 tablespoons extra virgin olive oil

a testo or heavy-based skillet

makes 8 muffins

In a bowl, cream the fresh yeast with the sugar and whisk in the hand-hot water. Leave for about 10 minutes until frothy. For dry yeast, follow the manufacturer's instructions. Sift the flour, cornmeal, and salt into a large bowl and make a well in the center. Pour in the yeast mixture and olive oil. Mix together with a round-bladed knife, then your hands, until the dough comes together.

Tip the dough out onto a lightly-floured work surface, wash and dry your hands, then knead the dough briskly for 5–10 minutes until smooth, shiny, and elastic—5 minutes for warm hands, 10 minutes for cold hands! Try not to add any extra flour at this stage—a wetter dough is better. If you feel the dough is sticky, flour your hands and not the dough. The dough should be quite soft. If it is really too soft to handle, knead in a little more flour.

To test if the dough is ready, roll it into a fat sausage, take each end in either hand, lift the dough up and pull and stretch the dough outwards, gently wiggling it up and down—it should stretch out quite easily. If it doesn't, it needs more kneading. Shape into a neat ball. Put in an oiled bowl, cover with plastic wrap or a damp kitchen towel and let rise in a warm place until doubled in size—about 1½ hours. Heat the testo or heavy-based skillet on the stovetop until medium hot.

Uncover the dough, punch out the air, then tip out onto a lightly-floured work surface. Divide into 8 smooth balls, then flatten each into a disk about ½-inch thick. Slide 2 or 3 disks onto the hot testo or skillet and cook for about 2 minutes on each side until risen and deep brown on the underside. Keep the cooked muffins warm and soft in a folded napkin or loosely wrapped in foil in a warm oven while cooking the rest. They are best served warm and eaten on the same day.

Almost like little muffins, these tiny treats hide a surprise when you bite into them—a cherry tomato bathed in pesto and melting mozzarella. Make them in advance and when you are ready to enjoy them, reheat in a warm oven.

little stuffed focaccia muffins

½ recipe Deep-Pan Focaccia (page 21), making just 1 ball of dough, risen twice but uncooked

8 tablespoons fresh pesto

1 ball of mozzarella, squeezed of excess water and diced

24 small cherry tomatoes

olive oil, for brushing

a few fresh thyme or rosemary sprigs, to garnish

coarse sea salt or rock salt, to sprinkle

a round cookie cutter, 3 inches diameter (optional) 2 x 12-cup mini-muffin pans, oiled

makes about 24 muffins

Preheat the oven to 400°F.

Uncover the dough, punch out the air, and divide it into 4 pieces. Roll or pull each piece as thinly as you can on a well-floured work surface.

Using a cookie cutter or an upturned glass, stamp out 6 small circles from the dough. Place a teaspoon of pesto in the middle of each circle, add a little mozzarella, then top with a cherry tomato. Bring the sides up and over the tomato and pinch to seal. Repeat with the remaining dough and fill ingredients to make a total of 24 muffins.

Put the muffins, sealed-side down, in the prepared mini-muffin pans. Brush the tops with a little olive oil, push in a herb sprig, and sprinkle with coarse sea salt.

Bake for 10–15 minutes until risen and cooked through. Tip out of the pans and eat warm, as a snack with drinks. Best eaten on the same day but can be reheated just before serving, if liked.

These coccoli ("little darlings"!) are a type of savory donut flavored with pancetta. I add lightly crushed fennel seeds, a flavoring that is very popular in Tuscany, especially with cured pork. Make sure they are piping hot and sprinkled liberally with coarse sea salt when you serve them. You can grind fennel seeds over them for a special finishing touch.

pancetta and fennel puffs

¾ cup milk

1¾ oz pure lard, roughly chopped

1½ cakes compressed yeast or 1 package quick-rising dry yeast

3½ cups Italian "00" flour or unbleached all-purpose flour

a good pinch of fine sea salt

2 oz. pancetta, finely diced

1 teaspoon fennel seeds, lightly crushed

vegetable or light olive oil, for deep-frying

coarse sea salt or rock salt, to sprinkle

a deep-fat fryer

makes 30-40 puffs

Put the milk and lard in a saucepan and heat gently until the lard has melted. Don't let the milk get too hot. Crumble in the fresh yeast (if using) and whisk until dissolved.

Sift the flour and the fine sea salt into a bowl and make a well in the centre. If you are using quick-rising dry yeast, stir it into the flour now. Pour in the warm milk mixture and add the pancetta and fennel seeds. Mix to a soft dough, adding more flour, if necessary. Form into a ball, cover with plastic wrap or a damp kitchen towel and let rise in a warm place for 2 hours or until doubled in size.

Heat the oil in a deep fat fryer to 350°F. A piece of stale bread dropped in should sizzle and turn golden in a few seconds.

Uncover the dough, punch out the air, and knead for 1 minute. Pull off small walnut-sized pieces of dough, about ¾ inch, and roll into rough balls. Fry in batches for about 2–3 minutes each, until pale brown and puffy.

Remove with a slotted spoon and drain on paper towels. Sprinkle with coarse sea salt and serve whilst still hot. Best eaten on the same day.

These crisp little circles of fried pizza dough topped with a blob of tomato sauce, mozzarella, and fresh basil, are often served in bars in Naples with your aperitivi. Although best served straight from the pan, you can make the puffy pizza bases beforehand, let them cool and store in an airtight container. To reheat, put them in a preheated oven at 350°F for 2–3 minutes, then add the toppings and serve. A wok makes a perfect fryer for these.

little fried Neapolitan pizzas

½ recipe Basic Pizza Dough (page 18), making just 1 ball of dough

⅔ cup any tomato pizza sauce

1 ball of mozzarella, squeezed of excess water and cut into tiny sticks

12 fresh basil leaves

vegetable or light olive oil, for deep-frying

a round cookie cutter, 3 inches diameter (optional)
a wok or deep-fat fryer

makes about 12 mini pizzas

Uncover the dough, punch out the air, and roll or pull it very thinly on a well-floured surface. Using a cookie cutter or an upturned glass, stamp out 12 or more 3-inch circles.

Heat the oil in a wok or deep-fat fryer to 375°F or until a tiny piece of dough sizzles instantly when dropped in. Deep-fry the pizzas, 4 at a time, for 2–3 minutes or until puffed and golden. You will have to turn them now and again so that they color evenly. Remove with a slotted spoon and drain well on paper towels.

Top with a little tomato sauce, a stick of mozzarella, and a basil leaf. Best served immediately whilst still hot.

These tiny rounds of dough, flavored with chopped scallions or sun-dried tomatoes or herbs, are made and baked in minutes. Serve as a nibble with drinks or an appetizer, with olives, salami, prosciutto, soft cheese, and your favorite selection of antipasti from the Italian deli.

little scallion breads

1 cup self-rising white flour

¼ teaspoon fine sea salt

2 scallions, finely chopped

2 tablespoons extra virgin olive oil

1 large egg

2 teaspoons sesame seeds

freshly ground black pepper

a round cookie cutter,
2 inches diameter (optional)

a baking sheet, lightly greased

makes 12 very small rolls

Preheat the oven to 375°F.

In a large bowl, mix the flour with the salt, 3 grinds of pepper, and the scallions. In a separate bowl, whisk the olive oil with the egg and 1 tablespoon water, then add to the dry ingredients. Work the mixture with your hands to make a soft dough. If there are dry crumbs in the bowl, add more water 1 teaspoon at a time.

Turn the dough out onto a lightly-floured work surface and knead for 10 seconds to make a smooth ball. Cover with a damp kitchen towel and leave for a couple of minutes. Knead for a couple more seconds, then roll out to about ¼-inch thickness. Stamp out rounds with a cookie cutter or an upturned glass and set slightly apart on a baking sheet. Gather up the trimmings and re-roll them, then cut out more rounds. Sprinkle with the sesame seeds and bake for 8–10 minutes or until golden brown and firm to the touch.

Serve warm from the oven. Best eaten the same day but can be frozen for up to 1 month. Thaw and gently reheat before serving.

variation:
Omit the scallions and use either 1 rounded tablespoon chopped sun-dried tomatoes or 1 tablespoon snipped chives or freshly chopped flatleaf parsley.

grissini and crisp breads

Schiacciata is a dialect word meaning "flattened", so pizza is sometimes known as schiacciata, i.e. a flattened bread dough. After making pizza one day, I had some dough left over and devised this "pizza" using leftover olives. There is no olive oil needed here, but you can have some really good olive oil in a little pot ready for dipping the hot pizzas into.

crispy olive 'pizza'

1 recipe Basic Pizza Dough (page 18) or any leftover dough

a splash of white wine

a handful of green olives, pitted and roughly chopped

coarse sea salt or rock salt, to sprinkle

extra virgin olive oil, to serve

a testo, terra cotta bakestone, or a large, heavy baking sheet

a large, rimless baking sheet

makes about 20-25 pieces

Preheat the oven to 425°F for at least 30 minutes. Put the testo, terra cotta bakestone, or a large, heavy baking sheet on the lower shelf of the oven.

Uncover the dough and punch out the air. Using a rolling pin, roll the dough out as thinly as you can, directly onto the baking sheet. Brush the surface with a little white wine, scatter with the olives, and sprinkle with coarse sea salt. Lightly press the olives and salt into the dough. Using a pizza wheel, score the dough in lozenge shapes directly on the baking sheet.

Bake for 5–10 minutes, until puffed and pale golden. Remove from the oven and break up into the pre-cut lozenges. Serve warm with olive oil for dipping and drizzling.

I bought a factory-produced version of this in Tuscany and it inspired me to bake my own. It's so easy to make that you quickly get into the rhythm of preparing it until it becomes second nature. Use any leftover dough that you might have.

crispy pizza sheets

1 recipe Basic Pizza Dough (page 18) or any leftover dough

2 teaspoons dried rosemary (optional)

extra virgin olive oil, to brush

sea salt flakes, to sprinkle

2 large, heavy baking sheets, lightly oiled

makes about 6 large pieces

Preheat the oven to 450°F.

Uncover the dough, punch out the air, and knead in the dried rosemary (if using). Divide the dough into 6 pieces and roll or pull it directly onto the prepared baking sheets. Press it out with your fingers as large and flat as you can. The dough should be so thin you can almost see through it—and it doesn't have to be even.

Brush it lightly with olive oil and scatter with sea salt flakes. Bake for about 8 minutes until golden, lightly bubbled, dry, and crisp. Shatter the sheets to serve.

We all know the paper packages containing a few grissini (breadsticks) which many Italian restaurants serve, but these are a more sophisticated version and can be made using leftover pizza dough. Just knead in the black pepper or any other flavoring that takes your fancy.

peppered grissini

½ recipe Basic Pizza Dough (page 18), making just 1 ball of dough

2 tablespoons cracked black pepper

2 tablespoons extra virgin olive oil

2 tablespoons butter, melted

a baking sheet, lightly greased

makes about 20 breadsticks

Make the pizza dough according to the recipe on page 18, adding the cracked pepper to the ingredients. Mix the olive oil and melted butter together. Before the first rising, roll or pull the dough into a thin rectangle, brush all over with the olive oil and butter mixture, and roll up loosely like a jelly roll. Flatten with the palm of your hand, then lift it onto a floured work surface. Cover with plastic wrap and let rise for 30 minutes.

Preheat the oven to 400°F.

Flatten the risen dough with your hand again to knock out the air, then roll out to a thickness of ¼ inch. Cut into long, thin strips and twist. Lay these onto a baking sheet and spray with water.

Bake for 5 minutes, spray again, then bake for a further 10–15 minutes or until golden and crisp. Keep an eye on them while they are baking as they can burn. Leave to cool on a wire rack and store in an airtight container for up to 1 week.

In Ligurian dialect, a ciappa is a thin, flat stone that has been used for baking flatbreads since the dawn of time. Nowadays these stones, made from a type of slate, are used to cook meat and fish at the table. A ciappa can also mean a slate roof tile, and has come to mean a thin, crisply baked cracker, reminiscent of the shape of these ancient Ligurian roof tiles.

ciappe "roof tiles"

1 tablespoon fine sea salt

6 tablespoons hand-hot water

2 cups Italian "00" flour or unbleached all-purpose flour

2 tablespoons extra virgin olive oil

2 large, heavy baking sheets

makes about 10 pieces

In a bowl, mix the salt with the warm water until dissolved. Sift the flour into a medium bowl and make a well in the center. Pour in the salty water and olive oil. Mix well, then knead the dough lightly for a couple of minutes until it is smooth. The dough should be firmer than pizza dough. Wrap it in plastic wrap and let rest for 15 minutes.

Preheat the oven to 350°F.

Divide the dough into 8. Roll or pull the pieces into long ovals. Roll them as thinly as you can and keep the work surface well floured to prevent sticking. Alternatively, you can use a pasta machine to roll them out if you are making a large quantity.

Lay the tiles on the baking sheets and prick all over with a fork with large tines. Make sure they are liberally peppered with holes.

Bake for 15–20 minutes or until evenly pale golden and dried out. Leave to cool on a wire rack and store in an airtight container for up to 2 weeks.

For all you anchovy-lovers out there, these are just the job. Transform leftover pizza dough into a savory snack by flavoring it with anchovies. The combination of these simple twists and a glass of chilled white wine truly transports you to a sunny terrace in southern Italy.

anchovy twists

½ recipe Basic Pizza Dough (page 18), making just 1 ball of dough

2 oz. canned anchovies in oil, drained and chopped

vegetable oil or light olive oil, for deep-frying

coarse sea salt or rock salt and cracked black pepper, to sprinkle

a wok or deep-fat fryer

makes about 15-20 twists

Uncover the dough, punch out the air, and knead in the anchovies. Roll or pull the dough out thinly and cut into long rectangles with a crinkled pastry wheel or a sharp knife. Make a slash in the middle of each rectangle, bring one end up and push through the slit, pulling it through loosely to make a roughly twisted shape.

Heat the oil in a wok or deep fat fryer to 375°F and deep-fry the twists in batches until golden and crisp. Remove with a slotted spoon and drain on paper towels. Sprinkle with coarse sea salt and cracked black pepper and serve warm.

The twists can be stored in an airtight container for up to 1 week. Reheat them for a few minutes in a warm oven when you are ready to enjoy them.

sweet breads

This is a rich, sweet, light-textured Italian breakfast bread flavored with oranges. It is made with pine nuts and hazelnuts in Southern Italy and with almonds in Sardinia. The nuts are gently toasted for maximum flavor.

pignola

scant 1 cup golden raisins

the finely grated peel and freshly squeezed juice of 2 oranges

2¾ cups unbleached all-purpose flour

1 teaspoon fine sea salt

1¼ sticks unsalted butter, diced

2 eggs, beaten

2 tablespoons hand-hot water

1 cake compressed yeast*

¼ cup hazelnuts, lightly toasted in a dry skillet

¾ cup pine nuts, lightly toasted in a dry skillet

confectioner's sugar, for dusting

a baking sheet, well greased

makes 1 large loaf

* To use active dry yeast, mix one ¼-oz. package with the flour after the butter has been rubbed in. Add the eggs and golden raisin mixture plus 2 tablespoons water; then continue as in the main recipe.

Put the golden raisins, finely grated orange peel, and juice in a bowl and let soak overnight.

Next day, mix the flour and salt in a large bowl. Rub the diced butter into the flour with the tips of your fingers until the mixture looks like coarse bread crumbs. Make a well in the center, then add the beaten eggs and the soaked golden raisin mixture.

Put the hand-hot water in a bowl, crumble the yeast over the top and mix to a smooth liquid. Pour into the well in the flour. Mix the yeast, eggs, and golden raisins together in the well, then gradually work in the flour to make a very soft, slightly sticky dough. If there are dry crumbs in the bowl, or the dough seems dry and tough, work in a little more hand-hot water, 1 tablespoon at a time.

Turn the dough out onto a floured work surface. Knead for 5 minutes. It will be soft and pliable but not as sticky. Return it to the bowl, cover with plastic wrap and let rise in a warm place until doubled in size, about 3 hours.

Turn the risen dough out onto a floured work surface, sprinkle with the nuts, and gently work them in. When they are evenly distributed, shape the dough into a ball, then pat into a round about 8 inches diameter and 1½ inches thick. Set on the prepared baking sheet. Slip the sheet into a large plastic bag, inflate slightly, seal, then let rise in a warm place until doubled in size, about 1 hour.

Preheat the oven to 375°F.

Uncover the dough and bake for 35 minutes or until the loaf is golden brown and sounds hollow when tapped underneath. Transfer to a wire rack, dust liberally with confectioner's sugar and let cool. Eat within 4 days or wrap in foil and freeze for up to 1 month.

This is a delicious bread to serve warm from the oven at breakfast time. I've used fresh black grapes here, but I have also made a lovely version using semi-dried Montepulciano grapes. If you wanted to try something similar, you could substitute semi-dried cherries or plump Lexia raisins. Serve it with salty cheeses such as Gorgonzola or Parmesan.

black grape schiacciata

⅓ cup extra virgin olive oil

a handful of fresh rosemary needles

3½ cups unbleached all-purpose flour or bread flour

1 teaspoon fine sea salt

2 tablespoons sugar

1 teaspoon quick-rising dry yeast

1 cup hand-hot water

14 oz. seedless black grapes

a deep baking pan, oiled

makes 1 medium loaf

Put the olive oil and rosemary in a bowl. Give the rosemary several good squeezes to release the aroma into the oil. Set aside for a few minutes.

Put the flour, salt, and 1 tablespoon of the sugar in a large bowl and stir well. Add the yeast and stir again. Pour in 2 tablespoons of the infused, strained olive oil and enough hand-hot water to make a soft but not sticky dough.

Turn the dough out on to a lightly-floured work surface and knead for 5 minutes, until the dough is smooth and elastic. Fold in the grapes and knead for a further 2–3 minutes. The dough may become sticky at this point, so dust with a little extra flour if necessary.

Press the dough into the prepared baking pan and push it with your knuckles to fill the pan. Let rise in a warm place for about 40 minutes, or until it has doubled in size.

Preheat the oven to 425°F.

Drizzle the remaining infused olive oil over the risen dough and scatter some of the rosemary needles and the remaining sugar evenly across the top. Bake for about 25 minutes or until the surface is golden brown and the base sounds hollow when tapped. Cool on a wire rack.

Eat on the same day or let cool completely, wrap in foil, and freeze. When you remove the bread from the freezer, thaw and wrap in foil, then reheat for 5 minutes in a hot oven.

This bread is delicious toasted for breakfast. Rather than spreading it with butter, try serving it with a sort of dressing which I make by whisking a little hazelnut oil and honey together with some grated orange peel. The bread is also lovely served with soft cream cheese.

fig and hazelnut breakfast bread

4 cups unbleached all-purpose flour or bread flour

2 teaspoons fine sea salt

¼ cup sugar

a ¼-oz. package of quick-rising dry yeast

2 tablespoons hazelnut oil

¾ cup hand-hot water

2 tablespoons blanched hazelnuts, toasted and chopped

10 oz. ready-to-eat dried figs, quartered

2 baking sheets, oiled

makes 2 small loaves

Sift the flour and salt into a large bowl and stir in the sugar. Add the yeast and stir again. Pour in the hazelnut oil and enough hand-hot water to make a soft but not sticky dough. Add the hazelnuts and figs and knead well to combine.

Turn the dough out onto a lightly-floured work surface and knead for 5–10 minutes. Divide into two rough loaves and put on the prepared baking sheets. Leave to rise in a warm place for about 1 hour, or until the dough has doubled in size.

Preheat the oven to 425°F.

Cut a couple of slashes in the top of each loaf and bake for about 25–30 minutes, until golden and firm, and the bases sound hollow when tapped. Cool on a wire rack.

Eat on the same day or let cool completely, wrap in foil, and freeze. When you remove the bread from the freezer, thaw and wrap in foil, then reheat for 5 minutes in a hot oven.

Mixing wheat flour with chestnut flour gives this bread a wonderful sweet and savory flavor that's almost smoky. It is generally made during the fall or winter months when chestnut flour is readily available. Serve it with Gorgonzola and pears and extra Vin Santo, of course.

chestnut and Vin Santo focaccia

4¼ cups Italian "00" flour or cake flour

1⅔ cups chestnut flour (*farina di castagne*)

1 teaspoon fine sea salt

1 cake compressed yeast, 1 package active dry yeast, or 2 teaspoons quick-rising dry yeast

⅔ cup extra virgin olive oil

⅔ cup Vin Santo mixed with 1⅓ cups water, warmed

coarse sea salt or rock salt, to sprinkle

2 cake, pie, or pizza pans, 10 x 1½ inches, lightly oiled

makes 2 focaccias

Sift both the flours and fine sea salt into a large bowl and make a well in the center. Crumble in the fresh yeast. For dry yeast, follow the manufacturer's instructions.

Pour in 3 tablespoons of the olive oil, then rub the oil into the flour and yeast until the mixture resembles fine bread crumbs. Pour the warmed Vin Santo and water into the well and mix until the dough comes together.

Tip out onto a lightly-floured work surface, wash and dry your hands, then knead the dough briskly for 10 minutes until smooth and elastic. The dough should be very soft, almost too soft to handle, but don't worry at this stage. Put in a lightly-oiled bowl, cover with plastic wrap or a damp kitchen towel and let rise in a warm place until doubled in size—about 1½ hours.

Uncover the dough, punch out the air, then divide into 2. Shape each piece into a round ball on a lightly-floured work surface. Roll out into two 10-inch circles and put in the pans. Cover with plastic wrap or a damp kitchen towel and let rise in a warm place for about 45 minutes or until very puffy and almost risen to the top of the pans.

Uncover the dough and, using your fingertips, make deep dimples all over the surface of the dough right to the base of the pan. Drizzle over the remaining olive oil, re-cover, and let rise for a final 30 minutes.

Preheat the oven to 400°F.

Spray the focaccias with water, lightly sprinkle with coarse sea salt, and bake for 20–25 minutes, until risen and golden. Transfer to a wire rack to cool. Eat on the same day or let cool completely, wrap in foil and freeze. When you remove the bread from the freezer, thaw and wrap in foil, then reheat for 5 minutes in a hot oven.